TREATISE WRITTEN TO A DEVOUT MAN

WALTER HILTON

CONTENTS

CHAPTER I

That he who intends to become a Spiritual Man must first use much Bodily Exercise in Penance, and in Destroying of sin

DEAR BROTHER IN CHRIST, --There be in the holy Church two kinds of life, by the which Christian souls do serve and please God, and procure their own salvation. The one is corporal, the other spiritual.

Corporal working appertaineth principally to the men and women of the world, who for the nature of their estate do lawfully use worldly goods, and intermeddle and deal with worldly businesses and affairs. This life also belongeth to all young beginners in spirituality who be but newly converted from sensual and worldly sins to the service of God; and this life is to dispose and enable such persons for spiritual working, by taming the body by corporal works and exercises, and thereby bringing it into obedience and subjection to the spirit, whereby it may become supple and ready, and not much contrarious to the spirit in her spiritual exercisings; for as St Paul saith, that woman was made for man, and not man for woman. Even so corporal working was ordained for spiritual, and not spiritual working for corporal. Corporal working is to go before, and spiritual working cometh after, as the same St Paul saith in these words: That is not first which is spiritual, but that which is sensible (or corporal), afterwards cometh that which is spiritual. And the reason why it should be so is this, that we are born in sin and in corruption of the flesh, by the which we are in souls so blinded and so overlaid that we neither have the spiritual sight or knowing of God by light of understanding, nor the spiritual tasting or feeling of Him by a clean desire of loving; and therefore we cannot suddenly start out of the dark night of this fleshly corruption into the spiritual light; for we are not as yet able to endure such spiritual light, by reason of the sickness of our souls, any more than we can with our bodily eyes, when they are sore, behold and look upon the light of the sun; and for that cause we must expect and work by degrees and process of time. First, by corporal works diligently, till we be discharged, or much lightened, or eased from this heavy burden of sin and sensuality, that hindereth us from spiritual working; and till our souls be somewhat cleansed from great outward sins, and enabled for spiritual workings.

By the corporal working that I speak of, thou must understand that I mean all manner of good works or deeds that thy soul doth by the senses or the members of thy body, either upon or towards thyself, as in fasting, watching, or in restraining thy fleshly or sensual desires, by penance-doing, or other acts of mortification. Or upon, or towards thy Christian brother, in performance of the works of mercy, spiritual or corporal. Or to, or towards God Himself, by suffering (for the love of Him and His justice) all manner of bodily pains and afflictions that shall occur for thee to undergo, either as immediately from His own hands, or by the means and from the hands of other creatures of His. All these kind of works done in faith and out of charity (without which they are of no worth) do please God. Therefore whoso desireth to become a spiritual man, it will be securest and profitable for him that he be first, for a long time, well exercised in these corporal workings, for these corporal deeds are practices and tokens of moral virtues, without which a soul is not able to work spiritually. Break down first pride within thee by bodily sufferings and bearings, and also by thinking in thy mind of something that will help to humble thee; and, moreover, by eschewing and avoiding all ostentations, boastings, or praising of thyself, either privately by thyself in thy mind, or by thy words or external deeds, or carriage towards, or with others; by this means casting away and mortifying within thee all vainglory and complacence in thyself for any talent, gift, or thing corporal or spiritual that God hath bestowed on thee. Also mortify and destroy within thee, so soon as thou art able, all envy and anger towards thy Christian brethren; whether they be rich or poor, good or bad, hate them not, nor disdain them, nor willingly offend them by words or by deeds. Likewise destroy and mortify in thee all coveting of worldly goods, and see that neither for the getting, or holding, nor saving of them, thou do not offend thy conscience, nor break verity with God, or thy Christian brother, for the love of any earthly thing; but what thou gettest, or hast, keep it without inordinate love or affection to it, and spend it as reasonable occasions shall require, for the honour of God, and the succour of thy Christian brother. Mortify also, and destroy as much as thou canst, all yielding to bodily sloth, and unnecessary bodily ease, and the sensual vices of gluttony and luxury, with the inordinations that rise out of them. And after that thou hast been well exercised and tried in all such kind of corporal works, thou mayest then by the grace of God, ordain thee and apply thee to spiritual working.

TREATISE WRITTEN TO A DEVOUT MAN

The grace and goodness of our Lord Jesus Christ, that He hath showed to thee, in withdrawing of thine heart from the love and liking of worldly vanity, and from the use of fleshly and sensual sins, and in turning of thy will entirely to His service, bringeth into mine heart much matter to love Him in His mercy; and also it greatly moveth and urgeth me to strengthen thee in thy good purpose, and in the work which thou hast begun between thee and God, so that it may be brought to a good end. And so far as may be in my power to help thee in it, my best endeavours in it I shall most willingly afford thee, first and principally for the service and honour of God, and next in requital of thy tender affection of love thou bearest to me, though I be a wretch, and unworthy of thy love or favour. I know well the desire of thy heart, as how that thou greatly covetest to serve our Lord both in soul and body, fully and wholly, without intermeddling or troubling thyself in worldly businesses, that so thou mayest, by the grace of God, attain to more knowledge, and spiritual feeling of God, and of spiritual things. Such desire of thine is (as I hope) good, and from God, for it is set upon Him in charity spiritually. Nevertheless, as in regard of external matters and workings in them, such desire of thine is to be moderated and ruled with discretion, according to the nature and quality of thy estate, which thou art to regard in thy spiritual intentions; for charity unruled, that is, not rightly ordered, turneth sometimes into a fault or vice. And therefore it is said of our Lord by a holy soul in the holy Scripture: He hath ordered charity in me; [1] that is to say, our Lord giveth to me charity, hath set it in order and good rule within me, whereby it might not err in its exercise, nor be lost through my indiscreet doings. Even so the said desire and charity which our Lord hath wrought in thee, out of His goodness and mercy, must be so ruled and moderated, that in the exercises of it, it do regard the nature of thy estate and condition of life, and the manner of living, which in former time thou hast held, and the measure and quantity of virtues that now are in thee. Thou must not altogether follow thy said desire in giving over or neglecting those businesses and cares of the world that are necessary, and do belong to thee, either for thee upholding of thy own person in his degree, or in the ruling or ordering of other persons or things that pertain to thy charge, and give thee wholly to retiredness, spiritual devotions and holy meditations, as if thou wert a Friar or Monk, or another man that were not bound (as thou art) to the world by children or servants; for it is not for thee to do so, and if thou dost, then keepest thou not the order of charity. Also if thou wouldst altogether leave and forbear all spiritual exercises (especially now after the grace and calling that God hath given thee for them) and give thyself wholly to the businesses of the world, in fulfilling of the works of the active life, as fully as do other men, that never felt such devotions nor had such grace or calling as thou hast, thou dost then leave the order of charity; for thy state requireth of thee to attend to each of them in divers times. Thou shalt mingle the works of active life with the spiritual works of the contemplative life, and then thou dost well; for thou shalt sometimes be busy, with Martha, for to order and govern thine household, thy children, thy servants, thy neighbours and thy tenants. If they do well, comfort and help them therein; if they do amiss, then tell and teach them for their amendment, and chastise them as there shall be cause. Thou shalt also wisely look after and know thy things and thy worldly goods, as that they be well and duly used or preserved by thy servants, well ordered and reasonably spent, whereby thou mayest the more plenteously, out of thy temporal means, fulfil the deeds of mercy and charity towards thy Christian brethren. Also thou shalt sometimes, with Mary, leave or lay aside the businesses of the world, and shalt sit down at the feet of our Lord with humility, in prayers and holy thoughts, and in Contemplation of Him, according to the grace that He shall give thee for it, and so thou shalt go from that one to that other, profitably and fruitfully, and fulfil them both; and so doing thou observest well the order of charity.

[1] Cant. 2:4.

CHAPTER II

To what kind of Men the Active Life pertaineth

BUT that thou mayest the less wonder at that that I have said, and that thou mayest better understand the reason thereof, therefore I shall declare the matter a little more fully to thee. Thou must understand that God is served by three kinds of life, as either by an active life, or by a contemplative, or by a third, that is mixed of them both, and therefore is commonly called a mixed life. The active life belongeth to worldly men and women that are gross and ignorant, as to the understanding or knowledge of spiritual exercises or ways, for they neither feel nor taste devotion by fervour of love as other men do, nor can they well conceive what it is or how it may be come by; and nevertheless, they have in them the fear of God and of the pains of Hell, and therefore they eschew and forbear sin, and have a desire for to please God, and to attain to Heaven, and a good will they bear to their Christian brethren. Unto these men it is needful and speedful to use the works of the active life as diligently as they can in the help of themselves and of their Christian brethren, for more they cannot do.

CHAPTER III

To whom the Contemplative Life appertaineth

THE Contemplative life appertaineth only to such men and women as for the love of God have forsaken all notorious sins, both of the flesh and of the world, and have given over all intermeddling with the affairs and businesses of the world, or with worldly goods, as also all care and charge over others, and all superiority or offices that concern the government of others (if ever they had any such) and make themselves poor and, as it were, naked from all the things of this life save for what their corporal nature doth merely need and of necessity require. Unto these men and women it appertaineth diligently and seriously to employ themselves in internal exercises for to get thereby (through the grace of our Lord) cleanness in heart and peace in conscience by destroying of sin and gaining of virtue, and so to come to Contemplation; since such cleanness (necessary for Contemplation) cannot be had without much exercise of body and continual travail or industry in spirit, by devout prayers, fervent desires and spiritual meditation.

CHAPTER IV

To whom appertained the Mixed Life

THE third kind of life that is called the mixed life belongeth to Prelates of holy Church and to pastors and curates who have charge and superiority over other men or women, for to teach and govern them, both as to their bodies and as to their souls, and principally to animate and guide them in the performance of the deeds of mercy both corporal and spiritual towards their Christian brethren. Unto these men of the mixed life it appertaineth sometimes to use the works of mercy in active life, in help and sustenance of themselves and of their subjects and of others also, and sometimes for to leave all manner of external businesses and to give themselves to contemplative exercises, as to prayer and meditations, reading of holy Scriptures or other good books or to some other spiritual exercises, according to what they shall feel themselves disposed. Also, this mixed life appertaineth to some temporal men, who are owners of much land and goods and have withal some dominion or mastership over other men, for to govern and sustain them, as a father hath over his children, and a master over his servants, and a lord over his tenants; the which men have received also of our Lord's gift, the grace of Devotion, and in some measure a taste and practice of spiritual exercise. Unto these men, I say, belongeth the foresaid mixed life, that is both active and contemplative; for if these men having (as they have) such external charge and cares lying on them, out of some obligation or necessity, would altogether leave or neglect such charge and businesses of the world pertaining to them, and give themselves wholly to the exercises of contemplative life, they would not do well in so doing, for they observe not the order of charity; for charity (as thou well knowest) consisteth in the love of God and of thy Christian brethren. And therefore he that hath charity in him, will not by occasion of his devotions, used immoderately towards God, omit that which he ought to do towards his Christian brother, but will serve both God and them for God, at divers times, as now the one and then the other; for he that for the loving of God in Contemplation leaveth the loving of his Christian brethren, and doth not perform towards them that which he ought, and is bound unto, he fulfilleth not the rule and obligation of charity. Likewise on the contrary side whoso hath so great a regard to the works of the active life and to the business of the world that for the love of his Christian brethren, and the serving of them, he leaveth or neglecteth all spiritual exercises, God having given him a call thereunto, he fulfilleth not charity, and so saith St Gregory. For though our Saviour Christ, for to stir up some to use the mixed life, took upon Himself the person of such manner of men, i.e., both of Prelates and of such other as are of the said mixed estate, and gave them example by His own working that they should upon occasion use the exercises of the mixed life, as He Himself did at those times that He spoke with men and meddled with them, showing and exercising His deeds of mercy towards them, taught the ignorant by His preaching, visited the sick and healed them of their diseases, fed the hungry and comforted the sorrowful; nevertheless, at other times He left the conversation of worldly men, and even of His own disciples, and went into the desert upon the hills, and continued there all night all alone in prayers, as the Gospel testifieth to us. And this mixed life did our Lord in Himself exercise, and show in the same manner, for an example to all other men that have taken on them the state or condition that requireth the exercises of the said mixed life, that is to say, that they should sometimes apply themselves to the external affairs and businesses belonging to their charge, and to the curing of such their Christian brethren as pertain to them to look to, instruct or provide for; and this to do according to reason and discretion and their need; and at another time to give themselves to devotion and to the exercises of a Contemplative life, being principally (as before I have said) reading and praying.

CHAPTER V

How holy Bishops held and used the said Mixed Life

THE said mixed life did holy Bishops hold and lead, who had charge over men's souls and had the ministration and disposal of temporal goods; for those holy men did not wholly forsake the administration looking to, and the disposal of worldly goods, and give themselves altogether, or unreasonably to Contemplation, notwithstanding the grace and gift they had for Contemplation; but very often left their own rest in Contemplation (which for their parts they had much rather have continued in still) for the love and service of their Christian brethren, and were contented to intermeddle with worldly businesses, for succouring and helping of those that were under their charge; and surely such doing of theirs was true charity. For justly and discreetly did they divide the time of their life into two parts, whereof the one they bestowed in the lower part of love and charity, that is to say, in the works of the active life (for they were bound thereto by taking on them their Prelacy): and another part of their time they spent in the higher part of love and charity, and that was in the contemplation of God, and of spiritual things by prayers and holy recollections; and so they had and held charity to God and their Christian brethren, both interiorly in affection of soul, and also exteriorly by doing and performing good corporal or external works. Other men that were only contemplatives, and were free from all cares and Prelacies, they also had charity towards God and their Christian brethren, but it was only interiorly in the affection of their soul, and not used outwardly in corporal deeds; and it may be it was so increased inwardly through their contemplations, that they needed not to intermeddle with external things for the bettering their charity, nor did it belong to their state of life to seek after such external workings, nor to intermeddle therewith, there being no necessity nor obligation for it on them; and so their internal charity sufficed for them. But those, whom before I mentioned, that were in Prelacy, and others also that were holy secular men, had perfect charity, both interiorly in their affection and did also exercise the same exteriorly in bodily working or deeds, and such doing is properly the mixed life which I have spoken of, consisting of the active and contemplative both together. And surely for such men that are in spiritual superiority, or have charge of the souls of others, as Prelates, Pastors and Curates have, or that are in temporal authority in the government of others, as worldly Lords and Masters are, I hold this mixed life best, and most expedient or necessary for them, so long as they remain in the said superiority and charge over others. But as for others that are free, and not obliged to any ministration or superiority, temporal or spiritual, I judge that the contemplative life alone by itself (if they have grace and calling to it) were, in truth, the best, the most expedient, most meritorious, most fair and most worthy for them to use, and not willingly to leave it for any outward working of the active life, unless it were in case of great need, as for the helping or comforting of some other men, either in their bodies or in their souls; and need requiring it, he to go about the doing of it, either when the party, or some other for him, requesteth, and craveth at his hands the doing of it; or that himself sees a mere necessity in the case, or else (being religious) when he is bidden by his superior to undertake or intermeddle with the work.

CHAPTER VI

That kind of Life was most fitting for him for whom this Treatise was made

BY that which I have said thou mayest partly understand the differences between one and another of the aforesaid three kinds of lives; and thou mayest by what I have said also judge which of them best fitteth thee, since that our Lord hath ordained and set thee in a state of superiority (of such nature as it is) and authority over others, and hath lent thee some store of worldly goods and lands, by the which thou mayest not only maintain and sustain thyself, but also all those other special persons that are under thy authority and government, and mightest withal govern them according to thy best knowledge and ability; and therewith also thou hast, through the goodness of our Lord, received from Him the grace for to know thyself, and a spiritual desire and taste of His love. I am of the mind that the life which I have termed to be mixed is best and most befitting thee; and thou accordingly to divide and dispose of thy time wisely and to the satisfaction of the foresaid rule of charity. For know thou well that if thou leave the necessary business or the active life belonging to thee, and be careless, and take no heed of thy worldly goods as how they be kept or spent, nor lookest after those that pertain to thy charge to see they do well, nor wilt afford thy help upon the necessity of thy Christian brother by reason of thy love and desire thou hast to apply thyself only to solitude and spiritual exercises, imagining that by so doing thou art excused and freed from thy foresaid obligations. If, I say, thou do so, thou dost not wisely nor profitably for thy soul; for what are thy works or exercises worth (be they spiritual or corporal) unless they be done according to justice and reason, to the honour of God and agreeable to His will? surely they are even nothing worth. Therefore if thou leave or neglect that thing which thou art bound unto by the law of charity, justice or other obligation, and wilt entirely give thee to another thing, voluntarily taken on thee, under pretense of better pleasing and serving of God, in a thing which thou art not bound unto, in so doing thou dost no discreet or acceptable service to Him. In so doing thou art careful to do honour and worship to His head and to His face, and to deck and adorn them fairly and curiously, but thou neglectest and leavest His body, with the feet, ragged and rent, and takest no care nor heed of them, nor dost thou anything honour Him; and it is but a shame and an indignity and no kind of honour for a man to be curiously dressed and decked about his head with pearls and precious stones, and therewith to have all his body naked and bare, as it were a beggar. Even so spiritually, it is no honour to God for one to crown His head and leave His body bare; for thou must understand that our Lord Jesus Christ, as a man, is the head of His spiritual body, which is the holy Church, the members or limbs of His body are all Christian men, some are arms, some are feet, and some are other members, according to the qualities, condition or estates they are of in the holy Church.

And now if thou be diligent with all thy skill and ability for to deck and adorn His head, that is, for to honour Him with the remembrance of His passion and of His other works done in His humanity, with devotion, love and thanks to Him for the same, and forgettest or neglectest His feet (which are thy children, thy servants, thy tenants and all thy Christian brethren) and lettest them to decay or perish for want of looking to, or to want clothing sufficient, or other necessaries, or otherwise not looked unto and provided for as they ought to be, then dost thou not please Him, nor doest Him any honour; thou seemest to kiss His mouth by devotion and spiritual prayer, but thou treadest upon His feet, and defilest them, inasmuch as thou wilt not tend to them (through thy negligence) that belong to thy charge and care. This is my opinion and advice to thee in this point; nevertheless if thou be of the mind that I say not aright in this matter, for that thou thinkest it were a fairer and more pleasing office to God for to do honour to His head, as to be all day devoutly thinking of His passion, and producing acts of inward affection upon it, than for to go home to other works that are more external, and make clean His feet, as for to employ thyself both in words and deeds about the helping or benefiting of thy Christian brethren, in so thinking thou thinkest amiss, and mistakest. For surely he will more thank thee and reward thee for the humble washing of His feet when they are very foul, and yield an ill savour to thee, than for all the curious painting and fair dressing or decking that thou canst make about His head, by the devoutest remembrance of His humanity; for it is fair enough, and needeth not much decking or dressing from thee; but for His feet, and other His limbs, that are sometimes ill-arrayed, and have need to be holpen by thee (namely, since thou art bound thereto), our Lord will render thee more thanks, if thou wilt humbly and charitably look unto them.

For the lower or meaner that the service which thou dost to thy Lord seemeth to be, in regard they are performed towards His members, and not immediately towards Himself, yet doing it for the love of Him, when reasonable occasions or need require it, and that with a cheerful and humble heart, thou much more pleasest Him than in service immediately done to Himself with omission of these offices of need or charity towards thy Christian brethren. And that thou mayest be the more willing to go about such an employment, thou shalt do well to think that it is sufficient, and best of all for thee to be employed in the very least degree, and lowest estate of His service, especially since it is His will that it be so. For thou must think, that since He hath put thee into that charge and estate of life, that it is the very best for thee, and that thou canst not do better than in performing what belongs thereto in the best manner and with all the willingness and gladness of mind that thou art able.

This I tell thee not as though that already thou dost it not, and better too; but to the end that thou shouldst do it with more alacrity and cheerfulness by occasion of this my writing; and shouldst not think it much sometimes to lessen or forbear thy spiritual exercise for to go and deal in worldly affairs pertaining to thee and thy estate, as to the looking and seeing too, that thy goods be well kept and spent according to reason, looking to the behaviour of thy servants and thy tenants, and doing other good deeds towards thy Christian brethren according to thy ability and their need, but shouldst perform both these works and exercises, that is to say, the internal and external, at divers and several times, and with as good a will the one as the other, so far as thou canst. As for example, if thou hast been at thy prayer and spiritual exercise, that finished thou shalt go and busy thyself in some corporal or external doing concerning thy Christian brethren, and therefore spend reasonable time with willingness and gladness of mind. And after that thou hast been busily employed for a time about thy servants, and other men with whom thou shalt have occasions, and hast profitably spent with them so much time as shall be truly needful, thou shalt then break from these external doings, and shalt return again to thy prayers and devotions, which thou shalt perform according to the grace that God shall give thee for it; and so doing, thou, by the grace of our Lord, shalt put away and avoid sloth, laziness, idleness and vain rest, which often creep upon us through the deceitfulness of our nature, under pretense or colour of contemplation or other spiritual recollections; whereby we come to omit the performance of good and meritorious external affairs and businesses pertaining to us and our charge by the appointment or providence of God. And thus thou shalt be always in some good exercise or other, internal or external, by turns, and in their proper times.

CHAPTER VI

Therefore thou shalt do well to observe and do that spiritually, that is, in thy carriage in a spiritual life, which Jacob did in a matter that was only corporal or external. The holy Scripture telleth, how that Jacob, when he began to serve his master Laban, he coveted Rachel his master's daughter for her fairness to be his wife, and for the having of her he served seven years; but when he had thought for to have had her to his wife, he had first Leah, the other daughter, instead of Rachel, and afterwards he takes Rachel, and so he had both at the last. By Jacob in holy Scripture is understood an overcomer of sins; by those two wives are understood, as St Gregory saith, the two kinds of lives that are in the holy Church, which are the active life and the contemplative life. Leah is as much to say as labour and painful working, and betokeneth the active life. Rachel is as much as to say as a sight of the beginning, which is God, and betokeneth the contemplative life. Leah bore children, but she was sore-eyed. Rachel was fair and lovely, but she was barren. And now even as Jacob coveted Rachel for her fairness, and yet had her not when he would, but first took Lead and afterwards Rachel, even so, every man labouring, and heartily seeking (by compunction for his former great sins of the flesh and of the world) now to become a new servant to God in cleanness of good living, hath a great desire to have and come by Rachel, which is to have rest in spiritual sweetness, devotion and contemplation, for it is so fair, and so lovely a life, that in hope for to have it he determined with himself, by the grace of our Lord, for to serve Him with all his diligence and might; but oft-times when he thinketh to have Rachel, that is, rest in devotion, our Lord suffereth him to be well exercised and tried, either with the temptations of the world, or of the devil, or of his flesh, or else with some external businesses and doing, corporal or spiritual, in help or succour of his Christian brethren; and when he is thus well exercised, and in travails with Leah, and is well-nigh overcome, then our Lord giveth him Rachel, that is, grace and devotion, and rest in conscience, and then hath he both Rachel and Leah.

So shalt thou do, according to the example of Jacob, these two lives, active and contemplative, since God calleth and enableth thee for both, and use the one with the other of them. By the one life (which is the active) thou shalt bring forth the fruit of many good deeds in help of thy Christian brethren; and by the other shalt thou be made to become fair, clear-sighted and clean in the supreme brightness and beauty, which is God, the beginner and ender of all that is made, and then shalt thou be truly Jacob, and an out-goer and overcomer of all sins; and after that, by the grace of God, thy name shall be changed, as Jacob's name was, and turned into Israel, and Israel is as much as to say: a man seeing God. Therefore, if thou be first Jacob, and will discreetly use these two lives afterwards, in time thou shalt be Israel, that is, a true Contemplative, either in this life, if God will deliver thee, and make thee free from the charges and businesses which thou art bound to, or else after this life, fully and perfectly in the bliss of heaven when thou comest thither. A man shall desire a contemplative life, for it is fair and full of merit, therefore thou shalt ever have it in thy mind, and in thy desire; but thou shalt have in using active life, for it is both expedient and necessary. Therefore, if upon just occasions, either concerning thy children or thy servants or any other of thy Christian brethren, for their profit or their heart's ease, upon reasonable cause, asking it of thee, thou be put from thy rest in devotion, when thou hadst much rather stay still thereat, be not angry with them, nor heavy or sad within thyself, so far as thou art able to help it, nor afraid, as if God would be angry with thee, that thou leavest Him for any other business or doing, for He will not be angry but well pleased and delighted thou so do. And therefore in such a case readily leave off thy devotion of what kind soever it be, and go about the deed, being service to thy Christian brethren, and that as willing and readily, as if our Lord Himself had called and bidden thee to go about it. Do so, I say, and endure the difficulty thou findest in it for His love; and put away all grudging for it, so far as thou canst; as also all bitterness and offence taken against thy Christian brother for calling thee to the said employment.

CHAPTER VII

That a Man's Devotion sometimes will be the greater by reason of the outward Work which before out of Charity he had been in hand with

AND it may fall out sometimes that the greater trouble thou hast exteriorly had in doing of thy active works, the more inflamed desire shalt thou afterwards have to God and the more sight of God and spiritual things, through the grace of our Lord, in devotion when thou comest thereto; for it fareth thereby as if thou hadst a little coal of fire, and wouldst make a fire therewith, and make it burn; thou wouldst first lay to some sticks, and with them over-cover the coal so that there is as yet no show or seeming hope of fire by it; nevertheless when thou hast abiden awhile and afterwards blowest it a little, anon, suddenly there will arise out a great flame of fire, so that the sticks will be turned all into fire. Even so is it spiritually; thy will and thy desire that thou hast to God is as it were a little coal of fire in thy soul, for it giveth to thee somewhat of light and of spiritual heat; but it is very little that it giveth, for often it waxeth cold and turneth to a fleshly rest (or into a rest of flesh and sensuality) and sometimes into idleness and doing of no good; therefore it is expedient that thou put to sticks, that is, some works of the active life; and though it be so that those works do seem for a time to be a let to thy desire, so that it may not be so entire nor so fervent as thou wouldst it were, yet be not daunted nor troubled thereat, but abide and suffer awhile, and so blow at the fire; that is, first go and do thy works, and afterwards, go alone to thy prayers and devotions, and lift up thine heart to God, and pray Him that of His goodness He will accept thy works that thou doest and receive them to His honour and glory; hold them as nothing in thine own sight, nor to be of any worth save so far as God only out of His goodness shall vouchsafe to accept of them; humbly acknowledge thy wretchedness and frailty really attributing thy good deeds to Him; and so much as they have any goodness in them, and inasmuch as they are bad, or not done discreetly with all circumstances requisite for a good deed, ascribe them to thyself, and then for this humility shall all thy good deeds turn into a flame of fire as do sticks laid upon a coal; and thou thus doing, thy external good deeds shall not hinder thy devotion but rather increase it. And moreover, our Lord saith in holy Scripture thus: Fire shall always burn in My Alter, and the Priest rising up in the morning shall put wood thereunto, so that the fire may not be extinguished. [2] This fire is love and desire to God in a soul, the which fire requireth that it be nourished and maintained by laying to sticks, so that it may not go out; and these sticks are of divers matters, as some of one kind of wood and some of another. A man that is learned and hath some understanding in the holy Scripture, if he have this fire of devotion in his heart, it is good for him to get him sticks of holy examples and devout prayers, and nourish the fire with them. Another man that is unlearned cannot so readily have at hand the sayings of holy Scripture, or of Doctors for the purpose, and therefore it is necessary for him to do many good external deeds to his Christian brethren, and thereby maintain and exercise towards them the love he beareth them for God.

And so it is good that each man in his degree, and according to what is most agreeable to the benefit and disposition of his soul, do get him sticks of one thing or another, as either by praying, considering, meditating or reading in some good and devout book, or in doing of some corporal or external work, thereby for to nourish in his soul the fire of love so that it may not become quenched; for the affection of love is dainty and tender, and will easily go out and vanish away unless it be well kept and continually nourished by good deeds or exercises, corporal or spiritual.

Now therefore, since our Lord hath put into thine heart a little sparkle of this blessed fire, that is Himself, (as holy Scripture saith, Our Lord is a consuming fire; [3] for, as a material fire wasteth all bodily things that may be wasted, so a spiritual fire, that is God, wasteth all kind of sin, and therefore our Lord is likened to fire wasting) I pray thee to nourish this fire within thee. This fire is nothing else but Love and Charity. This hath He sent into the earth, as He saith in the Gospel: I came to send fire into the earth, and to what end, but that it might burn? [4] that is, God hath put into man's soul a fire of love and a good desire, and a great good will for to please Him, and that He hath done to this end, that man should know it, keep it, and nourish it, and strengthen and increase it, and thereby be saved. The greater desire that thou hast to Him and for Him, the greater is the fire of love in thee, and the less that the desire is in thee, the less is the fire. The quantity or measure of thy desire within thee, how much it is, neither thyself doth know, nor doth any man know how great it is in him, much less the quantity of love that is in another man; God only knoweth it, or he to whom God shall reveal and make it known. And therefore dispute not with thyself as if thou wouldst know how great thy desire is; be busy and serious to desire as much as thou canst, but not to know the quantity or measure of thy desire.

[2] Lev. 6:12,13.
[3] Deut. 4:24; Heb. 12:29.
[4] Luke 12:49.

CHAPTER VIII

What the Desire of God for Himself is and how that in Cleanness of Conscience is found true Comfort and Sweetness

SAINT AUGUSTINE saith that the life of every good Christian man is a continual desire to God, and such desire is of great power and virtue, for it is a great crying in the ears of God; the more fervently thou desirest, the higher thou criest, the better thou prayest, and the wiser are thy thoughts. And what is this desire? Surely nothing but a loathing of all this worldly bliss, a forsaking of all fleshly or sensual love in thine heart, and an extreme loving, with a most hungry longing and thirsting after God and the everlasting bliss of Heaven; this is that which may be called a desire of God for Himself.

If thou hast this desire, as I verily hope and believe that thou hast, I pray thee keep it well and nourish it diligently; and when thou shalt pray or meditate of God, make this desire of Him to be the beginning and final intention of such thy exercises, and of all other thy works and deeds, thereby to increase it. Seek and nourish only this, and seek not after any feeling in thy corporal senses, external or internal, nor any sensible sweetness or devotion, neither by the ear nor by the taste of thy palate, nor by any wonderful light or sight of thy eyes, nor seek the sight of Angels, no, though our Lord Himself would appear in His body to the sight of thy eyes, make no great matter of that; and therefore let all thy diligence be that thou mayest truly and really perceive and find in thy soul, and especially in thy will, a loathing and full forsaking of all manner of sin and of all manner of uncleanness, with a spiritual seeing or perceiving how foul, how ugly and how painful these things be; and that thou mayest have within thee a mighty desiring of virtues, and, namely, of humility and charity, and finally, of the bliss of Heaven. This that I shall now tell thee were (as I would think) a spiritual comfort, and a spiritual sweetness in a man's soul; and that is, to have cleanness in conscience from wickedness and from all worldly vanities, with a firm faith and humble hope and a full desire of God. Howsoever it be for having of other comforts and sweetnesses I esteem that sweetness to be true, sound and secure that is found in cleanness of conscience, with a strong will of forsaking and loathing of all sins, and with inward sight and fervent desire of spiritual things; all other comforts and sweetnesses caused by any manner of feelings, unless they lead or help to the said end, that is, to cleanness of conscience and spiritual desire of God, are not secure to rest on.

But now thou wilt perhaps ask, whether this desire be love to God?

As to that I answer and say: That this desire is not properly love, but a beginning and taste of love, for love properly is a perfect uniting and coupling together of the lover and the loved into one. Perfect love maketh God and the soul to be as if they both together were but one thing. But such perfect coupling and union may not be had in this life, but only in desire and longing thereto, as by the example that I shall now deliver thee. If a man love another man that is absent, he greatly desireth his presence. Even so spiritually, as long as we are in this life, our Lord is absent from us, so that here we may neither see Him nor feel Him as He is, and therefore are not able (for want of such sight and feeling) here to love Him in fulness and perfection and in reality as we might do if we had the sight of Him really, and as He is in His own being; the which, because we have not, nor shall have in this life, therefore all that we can do here is to have a desire and a great longing and thirsting for to be present with Him and see Him in His bliss, and to be fully and perfectly united unto Him in love. This desire we may have in us (of His gift) in this life, by the which we shall be saved, for it is love unto Him, such as may here be had. St Paul saith thus: We know that while we are in this body we are pilgrims (or strangers) from God. [5] That is, we abide in this earth, or banishment, absent from Heaven, for we here walk by faith, and not by sight (that is, we here live in faith, not in real sight of Him as He is); but we are bold, and have a good will rather to be absent from the body, and to be present to our Lord (that is, we, through cleanness of conscience and sure trust of salvation, dare desire parting from our body by bodily death, and thereupon to be present to our Lord); nevertheless, because as yet we may not, therefore we endeavour, whether present or absent, to please Him; that is, we strive against the sins of the world, and pleasures of the flesh, and sensuality, by desire to Him, seeking to burn and consume in the fire of such our desire all things that may let or hinder us from Him.

But thou wilt perhaps further ask me: Whether a man may continually have this desire in his heart? and thou perhaps thinkest that he cannot.

As to that I will answer according to my opinion in it, which is, that thou mayest have this desire in thine heart and intention virtually or habitually, always and continually; but thou canst not so have it as to working or exercising upon it, as thou mayest better understand by this example. If thou wert sick, thou wouldst have, as every man in such a case hath, continually a natural desire in thine heart of bodily health; and this whether thou be asleep or awake, but art thinking of some worldly things; thou hast then such a desire only in intention or habit, and not in using or acting upon it. But when thou thinkest on thy bodily sickness or on thy health, then hast thou thy said desire of health in using and acting. Even so it is spiritually in the desire of God. He who by the gift of God hath this desire, though he sleep, or else thinketh not on God, but on some other worldly things, yet hath he this desire in his heart and soul till he commit some deadly sin. But as soon as he thinketh on God or purity of life or the joys of Heaven, then his desire to God worketh actually, as long as he keepeth his thought and intention to please God, either in prayers, meditations, or any other good action, so that all his endeavour be to excite this desire, and discreetly use it sometimes in one deed, sometimes in another, according as he is disposed and hath grace thereto.

This desire is the root of all thy actions that are rewardable. For whatever good deed thou doest for God's sake, whether it be bodily or spiritual, as when thou prayest or meditatest, it is an exercising and using of this desire. And therefore when thou doest any good work, scruple not whether thou desirest God or no, for thy deed showeth thy desire. Some ignorantly conceive that they desire not God except they be ever calling upon Him either with their mouths or their hearts; and therefore they are continually saying, Lord save me, or some such-like words; which words indeed are good, because they stir up the heart to a desiring of God. Yet nevertheless, without any such words, a pure thought of God, or any spiritual thing, or of virtue, or the humanity of Christ, or joys of Heaven, or understanding of the holy Scriptures, with love, may be better than such words. And the more spiritual thy thought is, the more is thy desire. Be not, therefore, in doubt whether thou desirest God, when thou thinkest upon Him or doest any outward good work to thy neighbour, for thy deeds show it. Nevertheless, though all thy good actions, spiritual and corporal, are a demonstration of thy desire to God, yet is there a great difference between spiritual and corporal deeds, for deeds of a Contemplative life are not so outward as the other; and therefore when thou prayest unto, or meditatest upon God, thy desire to Him is more entire, more fervent, more spiritual than when thou doest external works of charity to thy neighbour.

Now, if thou ask me by what means thou shalt keep this desire, and nourish it, I shall tell a little in that point, not with the meaning that thou shalt or must use the self-same form that I tell thee for it; but that thou thereby have some kind of general example, whereof thou shalt make use upon thy need and according to thy manner --not my manner, unless mine seem more for thy purpose, for I neither may nor can tell thee fully what is best for thee to use; but I shall tell thee somewhat according to what I think.

[5] 2 Cor. 5:6.

CHAPTER IX

How thou shalt Dispose thee to Devotion

IN the night after thy sleep, if thou wilt rise to pray and serve our Lord, thou shalt feel thyself at the first to be fleshly, heavy, and, as it were, drowned in sensuality, and ofttimes impertinent thoughts of the world or other vanities pressing into thy mind. But then shalt thou dispose thee to pray, or to think some good thought, for to revive and quicken thine heart towards God, and do thou use all thy discreet industry, for the drawing up of thy thoughts from worldly vanities, and from vain imaginations that come into thy mind, that so thou mayest feel some devotion in such vocal prayers as thou shalt then use, if thou use any such; or else (if thou wilt) enter thou into some spiritual thoughts, whereby thou mayest not remain hindered and troubled with such vain thoughts of the world or of thy flesh. And now as for matter of good thoughts for thee, thou must know that there be divers matters of such thoughts or meditations, but which of them were best for thee to take and use I cannot tell thee.

But I trow that such matter and manner of thinking or meditating, wherein thou feelest greatest gust, facility and ease or pleasure, is best for thee to use so long as it continueth so grateful to thy spirit. Thou mayest (it thou wilt) sometimes think on thy sins heretofore committed, and of the frailties into which thou daily fallest, and ask mercy and forgiveness for them. Also after this thou mayest think on the frailties and sins and miseries, corporal and spiritual, of thy Christian brethren, with pity and compassion of them, and ask mercy and forgiveness for them as tenderly as for thyself, and as if thou hadst done them, and that is a good exercise for the time. For I tell thee for truth that thou mayest make of other men's sins a precious ointment for to heal thine own soul, when thou thinkest on them with compassion and sorrow for them; this ointment is precious and very medicinal, though the spicery or things whereof it is composed be not clean, or otherwise wholesome; for it is treacle or mithridate, made of poison for to do away and destroy poison; that is to say, thine own and other men's sins. If thou beat and bruise them well with sorrow of thine heart, pity and compassion, they turn into treacle or mithridate, that will cleanse and make whole thy soul from pride and envy, and bring into it love and charity to thy Christian brethren. Such thought is good for thee sometimes to take into thee.

32

CHAPTER X

How a Man is to Think on the Humanity of Christ

ALSO for thy exercise of devotion thou mayest think on the humanity of our Lord, as of His birth, of His Passion or of any other of His works, and feed thy thought with spiritual imagination thereof, for to move thine affection more to the love of Him. This thought (I mean of something of our Saviour's humanity) is good and expedient, namely, when it cometh freely of God's gift, with devotion and fervour of spirit, else a man will not likely find taste or devotion in it. And if he have it not with such facility and sending of God, I think it not expedient that a man should much force himself in it, as if he would get it by violence; for so doing he might hurt his head and body too, and yet be never the nearer. Therefore I think that it is good for a man to have in his mind and thought sometimes our Saviour's humanity, or some matter thereof; and if devotion come withal, and relish or gust found in it, then to hold it and follow it for a time, but leave off soon, and hang not long thereon. And if devotion come not by thinking of the Passion, strive not, nor press too much for to have and come by such devotion or feeling in it, but take what will easily come; and if it come not easily betake thee to some other matter, wherein thou thinkest or hopest to find more devotion or gust.

CHAPTER XI

How a Man shall think on Virtues and upon the Saints

ALSO other thoughts there be that are more spiritual, as to think on virtues, and to see by light of understanding the virtue of humility, what it is, and what great reasons be why a man should be humble; and also what is patience, cleanness in soul, justice, charity, sobriety and other such like virtues; and how worthy it is that a man should labour for the getting of them, and of the means by which they may be gotten, and by such thoughts to have a great desire and longing to the having of those virtues; and also for to have a spiritual sight of the three principal, or Theological Virtues, Faith, Hope and Charity. By the sight and desire of these virtues a soul should see and feel much grace of our Lord, without which grace a man's soul is half blind, and without spiritual sweetness or taste. Also, for to think on the saints, as the apostles, martyrs, confessors and holy virgins, beholding in his interior their holy living and the grace and virtues that our Lord gave them in their life, and by the remembrance and consideration hereof, to stir thy heart for to take example from them for leading a better and perfecter life.

CHAPTER XII

How a Man shall think of the Holiness of our Lord Jesus and of our Blessed Lady

ALSO the thinking and considering (above all other saints) of our Lady St Mary and her excellency in grace and virtues is a good matter for raising and exercise of devotion, by seeing with thy spiritual eye the abundance of grace that was in her holy soul when she was here living, which our Lord had given her, above what He gave to any of the other Saints; for she was replenished with all other virtues, without one spot of sin, showing and manifesting by her life perfect humility and fulness of charity, with the beauty and excellence of all other virtues, the which virtues altogether make her so holy, that there would no temptation, or motion of pride, envy, wrath or anger, sensual delight or of any other kind of sin or imperfection enter into her heart or defile her soul in any part of it. By the beholding of the beauty and excellency of this blessed soul, a man's heart should be moved and put into a great spiritual delight and comfort.

And much more and above that is the beholding of the soul of our Lord Jesus, the which soul of His was fully and wholly united to the divinity, excelling without any comparison our blessed Lady and all other creatures. For in the Passion of Jesus are two natures, that is, God and man, perfectly united together. By the virtue of this most blessed union, which cannot be expressed nor yet conceived by man's wit or understanding, the soul of Jesus hath received the perfection and fulness of all wisdom and goodness; as the Apostle saith: The fulness of the divinity doth dwell is Christ corporally; [6] that is, the divinity of God was fully united to the humanity (or man's nature) in the soul of Jesus, and so, by the means of His soul dwelling in His body, the remembrance of the humanity of our Lord after this manner (that is, to regard the virtues and surpassing grace of the soul of Jesus) should be right comfortable to a man's soul.

[6] Col. 2:9.

CHAPTER XIII

Of seeing and beholding the Power (by some consideration or thinking), the Wisdom, the Goodness and the Mercy of God in His Creatures

ALSO the remembrance of the power, the wisdom and the goodness of our Lord in all His creatures; for as much as we living here on earth cannot see God fully and as He is in His essence, therefore we are to see and behold Him, love and fear Him upon the sight and consideration of His creatures and His works; and in them also are we to admire and wonder at His power and goodness. Also, for to think on the mercy of our Lord, that He hath showed to me and to thee, and to all sinful captives that sometimes were in bondage to the devil, through the greatness and multitude of our sins; how He patiently suffered us to live in our sin, and in our heinous contempts of Him, and work no revenge on us for the same, as He most justly might have done, and might most worthily have cast us down headlong into Hell, if His love had not hindered Him; but out of love He spared us, and sent His grace into our souls, taking us out of the state of heinous sins, and by His grace hath turned our will entirely unto Him, and made us thereby, for the having of Him, and for His love, to forsake all manner of sin. The remembrance of His mercy and goodness, in these and in other matters and points more and greater than I can now reckon up, may justly cause and bring into a soul a great truth and confidence in our Lord, and a full hope of salvation, and greatly inflameth the desire of love to aspire to the joys of Heaven.

CHAPTER XIV

How the Consideration and thinking on the Miseries and Perils of this Life is apt to breed in a soul the Desire of Heaven

ALSO to think upon the miseries, mischiefs and perils, corporal and spiritual, that happen in this life; and after that to think of the joys of Heaven, as how great happiness is there, and what wonderful joy and delight; for there is neither sin, nor sorrow, nor passion nor pain, hunger nor thirst, aches nor sickness, doubt nor fear, shame nor blame, nor want of power, nor strength, nor lack of light, nor coldness in love; but there is most excellent beauty, clearness, strength, health, everlasting delights, perfect wisdom, love, peace, honour, security, rest, joy and bliss in abundance without ever having any end. The consideration of these points ought to cause thee the more fervently to covet and desire those everlasting joys and rest of that same most blessed life. Many men are covetous of worldly goods, honours and earthly riches, and think both in dreaming and waking how and by what means they might come thereto; and then they forget all care of their souls' good, and all thoughts of the pains of Hell, or of the joys of Heaven. Surely these men are not wise; they are like to children that run after butterflies, and, because they look not to their feet, they sometimes easily fall down and break their legs. What is all the pomp, honours, riches and jollity of this world but a butterfly? Surely it is no more, yea, it is much less. Therefore, I pray thee, be covetous of the joys of Heaven, and thou shalt have honour and riches that shall last for ever. For at the latter day, when worldly covetous men bring no good in their hands (because all their honour and riches, which they only made account of, are turned into nothing but sorrow and pain) then the good men of the world, that have truly forsaken all vain honours and riches of this world, or else if they had them they made no account in their hearts of them, nor did set their love or delight in them, but have ever lived in the peace of God and in humility and in hope, and sometimes in sorrows or afflictions, and patiently expected the mercy of God; they (I say) shall then fully attain that which they here coveted, for they shall be crowned as kings, and shall ascend up with our Lord into the bliss of Heaven. Also there be many other good considerations or thoughts (more than I can speak of) that serve to stir and raise a man's mind and affection to loathe the vanities of this world and to desire the joys of Heaven.

These matters I have not mentioned unto thee as if I had withal fully showed the manner how they are exercised in a man's soul; but I have only touched them a little, to the end thou mightest, by so much the better, understand these things for such use as thou canst best make of them.

CHAPTER XV

How a Man shall do when he feeleth no taste nor comfort in his Mental Exercises

NEVERTHELESS I would think it were good for thee that when thou disposest thee to think on God, as I have before said, or in any other manner, and peradventure thou feelest no gust nor devotion in thy exercise, but only a naked mind and a weak will; by which thou wouldst fain think on God, but canst not; then I think it is good for thee that thou strive not too much with thyself, for so thou mayest fall into greater darkness, unless thou knowest how to work more subtlety, and more above in spirit, and with all quietness in the senses. But thou not knowing how to do so for want of experience or skill in it, I hold it more secure for thee in such a case for to say thy Pater noster and thine Ave Maria, or else thy Matins, or to read in thy Psalter, for that is evermore a sure standard that will not fail. Whoso may cleave thereto he shall not err; and if thou canst by thy prayer get devotion, look then that this devotion be only in affection, that is to say in a great desire toward God, with a spiritual delight. Hold on then such thy saying of those vocal prayers, and not easily break off; for oftentimes it happeneth that praying with the mouth getteth and keepeth devotion, and if in such a case thou cease from saying, thy devotion withal vanisheth away.

Nevertheless, if Devotion in prayer bring into thine heart a devout thought of the humanity of our Lord, or of any of the other matters before mentioned by me, and this thought should be hindered by thy saying of the vocal prayers, then will it be best for thee to cease from thy saying, and to feed thy mind and affection with the thought of the said good matter till it leave thee and be vanished away.

CHAPTER XVI

What a Man is to take heed of in his Prayers and Meditations

BUT of certain things it behoveth thee to beware in thy meditations; of some of them I shall tell thee. One is that when thou hast had a spiritual thought or imagination of the humanity of our Lord, or of other bodily things, and thy soul hath been comforted and fed therewith, and afterward it passeth away of itself; do not seek, as it were, by mastery or force to hold it still, for then it will turn thee into pain and bitterness. Also, if it pass not away, but dwell still in thy mind, without any travail or industry of thine, and thou, for the comfort thou findest in it, wilt not leave it, and thereupon it still continuing with thee, cometh to bereave or hinder thee of thy sleep at nights, or else in the day times hindereth thee from other good deeds, or else through the great fervour that it worketh in thy body, thy body or thine head by it falleth into a great feebleness, then must thou lessen or moderate, and sometimes forbear such exercise of thine, even when thou hast most devotion in it, or to it, and wouldst otherwise be most loth to forbear it, or part from it; and therefore thou must needs use discretion in the matter, for to avoid those mischiefs, or any of them, which now I have reckoned up to thee, or any other mischief or peril that may come to thee through indiscreet fervour or love to those thy exercises; and in particular, give it over when it is reasonable time to give it over, or when thy Christian brother may receive harm, or take just offence at thee by occasion of thy long stay at such thy devotions. If thou do otherwise in this matter than I have told thee, I think thou dost not well nor wisely in it.

A worldly man or woman that peradventure feels not devotion twice in a year, if he (through the grace of our Lord Jesus) feel great compunction for his sins, or think seriously or devoutly on the Passion of our Lord, or upon any other good matter, if he by occasion thereof, and his devotion therein, be put from his sleep and his rest, for one, or two, or three nights, until his head ache, it makes no great matter, nor will he be the worse for it; such devotion cometh but seldom upon such persons. But as for thee, or any other man or woman, that every day duly performest, or hath such devotions, and intendest to continue in pursuing of such daily exercises, it is expedient for thee to use and hold discretion in thy performance of those thy exercises, and not fully to yield and plunge thyself into devotion, so far as it will offer itself unto thee, but moderate thyself in it, and take it moderately, though it offer itself to thee in abundance.

Also I hold it good, that thou observe this discretion in thy exercise, which is, that thou tarry not too long at it, that thereby thou put thyself from taking thy meat or of thy sleep, when the time shall be for taking of them, or do give just cause of displeasure or damage to any other man, through occasion of overlong tarrying at such thy devotion. The wise man saith: That all things have their time. [7]

Another thing which behoveth thee to beware of is that when thy mind hath been employed for a time in the imagination of the humanity of our Saviour, or any other good matter, and after this thou seekest with all the desire of thine heart, for to have a more spiritual knowing or feeling of the divinity; press not too much upon such desire, nor suffer the desire of thine heart to tarry too long therein, as if thou wert expecting and tarrying for some better or higher elevation of thy spirit, or for a feeling that had more worth or excelling in it than any thou hast hitherto had. Thou shalt not do so. It is enough for thee and for me for to have a desire and a longing to our Lord; and if He out of His grace and goodness will vouchsafe, over and above such desires of ours, freely, and of His own accord, to send us of His spiritual light, and open our spiritual eye, for to see or know more of Him than heretofore he did or could, by our own labour and industry, let us thank him for it; but if He do not (because we are not as yet humble enough, but were likely to grow proud by reason of such extraordinary favours, if He bestowed them on us, or are not disposed in other respects, and namely, by cleanness of conscience through well living, for to receive such grace and favour at His hands), then let us humbly acknowledge our own unworthiness, and hold ourselves satisfied with the desire we have of Him, and with other common good thoughts, that may easily be had and used by our imagination; as thinking of our sins, of Christ's Passion, or other such like things, or else with some vocal prayers of the Psalter or other vocal prayers, and thank Him with all our hearts, that He bestoweth upon us any portion of His grace or favour, though it be the least that any man hath. And if thou do otherwise, thou mayest easily be deceived (for thy presumption) by the spirit of error; for it is a great folly for a man of his own head or wilfulness to press or strain himself too much, to get into the sight or exercise of spiritual things further than he seeth well that he hath invitation and enablement for it. For the wise man saith that the searcher of the Majesty (of God) shall be oppressed by the glory of Him; [8] for not having humility, cleanness and worthiness in soul, for such a sight he shall be cast down, and made to know himself better than he did through this confusion. And therefore the same wise man in another place saith thus: Do not seek for things that are higher, nor search into things that pass thy strength; [9] that is to say, high things that are above thy natural reason and apprehension seek not after, and great matters that are above thy ability or strength do not search into. By these words the wise man doth not wholly forbid us to seek after and desire the knowing and having of spiritual and heavenly things, but he forbiddeth us to seek for them in a preposterous manner, which is too soon, and sooner than we are fit for them or that God calleth us to them, as when we are as yet sensual, and not cleansed from the vain love of the world; being in that degree, we are not to take upon us as if we could or would by our labour or industry, or by our own wit, enable ourselves to discern, see or know spiritual things, or procure in us great fervour of the love of God; so that albeit we see that we set at nought all worldly things, and it seem to us that we would for God's love forsake all the wealth, honour and joys of this world; yet for all this we are unfit and indisposed for to seek and behold spiritual things that are above us, until our souls through precedent exercises of the imagination, become to be more subtle, or as it were thin, or somewhat spiritual, and withal he become well mortified and settled in virtues by process of time and by increase in grace. For (as St Gregory saith) no man suddenly (or hastily) becometh supreme or perfect in grace, but beginneth with little, and proceedeth on by little and little, until that he come to be perfect, the which God grant that we all may one day be. Amen.

FINIS.

[7] Eccles. 3:1.
[8] Prov. 25:27.
[9] Ecclus. 3:22.